WEST COUNTY

WEST COUNTRY WANDERINGS IN POETRY

Doreen Beer

ARTHUR H. STOCKWELL LTD
Torrs Park, Ilfracombe, Devon, EX34 8BA
Established 1898
www.ahstockwell.co.uk

© Doreen Beer, 2018
First published in Great Britain, 2018

The moral rights of the author have been asserted.

All rights reserved.
No part of this publication may be reproduced
or transmitted in any form or by any means,
electronic or mechanical, including photocopy,
recording, or any information storage and
retrieval system, without permission
in writing from the copyright holder.

British Library Cataloguing-in-Publication Data.
A catalogue record for this book is available
from the British Library.

By the same author:
Poems from a Devon Village
Poems from the English Countryside
Through Nature's Voice

ISBN 978-0-7223-4886-4
Printed in Great Britain by
Arthur H. Stockwell Ltd
Torrs Park   Ilfracombe
Devon EX34 8BA

CONTENTS

The Heartbeat of Devon	9
To My Gran	10
April	11
Then and Now	12
Foxgloves	13
Preserving Jerusalem	14
Seashells	15
On Sidmouth's Cliffs	16
The Oaken Gate	17
I am a Song	18
The Lamb	19
Life's Rugged Road	20
Optimism	21
Time's Mockery	22
The Water Babies	23
The Garden Guest	24
The Vital Spark	25
How Good This Earth Could Be	26
The Rock	27
The Crow's Lament	28
The Dance of Devonshire	29
Supreme Plan	30
Time to Wonder	31
Things That Count	32
The Wild Ones	33
Devonshire Is Poetry	34
The Watchers	35

Far from the Madding Crowd	36
Knowing	37
Winter's Replenishment	38
Blustery Day	39
The Owl's Tale	40
Lost Meadowlands	41
Birds in a Storm	42
Untrodden Snow	43
Master of the Plot	44
Seagulls at Shaldon	45
A Country Dog Show	46
While I – Even I	48
Flower-Arranging Classes in November	49
The Lonesome Pine	50
A Pig's Reprieve at Pennymoor	51
Happy Wanderers	52
Gone with the Wind	53
Springtime Blesses All	54
Christmas Eve	55
The Stricken Ash at Bickleigh	56
The Last Rosebud	57
Granny's Old Black Crock	58
Enchantment	60
The Message of the Rose	61
The Days of Steam	62
The Village Churchyard	64
Bleak House	65
Gather Such Treasure	66
A Village Owl and Pussycat Tale	68

On the Line	70
The Lights of Life	71
Celebrations	72
Heart's Truth	74
A Wartime Memory	75
Village Barber/Bell-Ringer	76
Grandmother's bed	78
A Most Precious Partridge	79
Back to Basics	80
Like an Ember	82
The Spirit of the River	83
Bird Talk	84
So Great a Heritage	86
Remembering Diana	87
When Wild Cherries Blossom	88
Heart of a Rose	89
The Wind in the Willows	90
West Country Moorlands	91
Ticket to Ride	92
Did They Know?	93
New Year	94

The Heartbeat of Devon

The conception of its heartbeat
Began neath Devon's dark peat;
Throbbing quietly at first,
It louder grew and knew a thirst,
So took the water of a spring
To fuel its beat, and through the ling
It pulsed and gushed and sought a course
Through whortleberry, fern and gorse;
Out of the spring a stream did grow
And added waters to its flow.
Ever wider, ever longer
Devon's heartbeat pulsed much stronger
Ensuring life throughout the county
Enriching all its glorious bounty.

To My Gran

Dearest Gran, you'll not read this
For I've written it too late.
In your lifetime I was young
Poetry had had to wait;
But now I've children of my own
And your ways to them explain,
You're in my heart, my dearest Gran,
And you live through them again.

My thoughts of you, though adult now,
All from my childhood spring –
The holidays with you I spent,
You taught me how to sing;
You taught me to be happy
With the simple things of life,
The joy in cooking, sewing, knitting
That makes a good housewife.

Although you raised nine children,
And times were hard ones then,
I'm sure if you relived your life
You'd choose the same again,
For true contentment was your virtue,
Luxuries not yours to know,
So your life inspired this poem,
Because I loved you so.

April

Blithely April dances
Upon the greening lawn,
Sprinkling it with daisies
Dipped in the dews of dawn.
Sweetly her breath pervades
The gentle springtime breeze,
As violets are secreted
Beneath the stirring trees.

Into nooks and crannies
She tucks primrose posies fair
While blackthorn and wild cherry
Are bedecked in bridal wear.
Birdsong echoes forth
In joyfulness on high,
That winter's icy footsteps
Have at last passed by.

Yet April is oft-times fickle
And as tulip torches show,
She may show a change of face
And powder them with snow.
Thus her days are swiftly spent
And her hours soon ebb away,
In time to wake the bluebell glades
To be glorified by May.

Then and Now

Mr Then and Mr Now
Never seem to meet somehow,
For Mr Then lived in the past
And Mr Now will never last –
Not for a day, not for a week
And so these two will never speak.

Of Mr Then we converse much,
Granting him the perfect touch
For making all our lives ideal –
Was he too good to be quite real?

Mr Now, he begs us borrow
Our joy and pleasure from tomorrow;
Neither of them may we keep,
So for the present we will sleep,
Weaving our dreams of Now and Then,
Those enigmatic Mr Men.

Foxgloves

A sweep of foxgloves flowing wide,
Magenta-hued a whole hillside,
Nodding, bowing in the breeze,
A pollen paradise for bees.
What a glorious sight to see,
When viewed quite unexpectedly:
To capture upon camera
This beauteous scene we yearned,
And for such a purpose the next day we returned
To feast our eyes and memorise
In gladsome summer hours
This lovely vibrant gathering –
A whole platoon of flowers.

Preserving Jerusalem
(inspired by Blake)

And will our feet in future times
Walk among England's woodlands green?
And will we thank our heavenly God
For England's pleasant pastoral scene?
And will His countenance benign
Smile down upon those open meads?
And will Jerusalem yet exist
If endless road building proceeds?

Bring me a pen that I may write,
Bring me a heart with true desire,
Give me the will thus to incite,
Bring me companions who aspire;
We will not cease our yearly fight
Nor shall we penned petitions scorn,
'Til we've preserved Jerusalem
For England's children yet unborn.

Seashells

Such intricacy amazes
One who simply stands and gazes,
A Creator so divine
Surely fashioned such design.
Subtle differences in all,
With complex patterns to enthral.
Flowers of earth, birds and trees
Daily lift our hearts, to please
The artist, that in mankind dwells;
But look – and really look – at shells,
So wonderfully each one is made,
Never to glorify earth's glade,
But destined for the oceans vast,
Eyed solely by fish shoals that pass,
And when their life within is o'er
Launched by waves upon the shore,
To be collected by the hand
Of the stroller on the sand,
The one who simply stands and gazes
At this creation which amazes.

On Sidmouth's Cliffs

An eerie wintry wildness
Captured the summer sea
And held me fascinated
By its awesome majesty.
Something of its turbulence
Affected me and though
I had no wish to linger,
Away I could not go.

But in a trance of wonder gazed,
As white horses, row on row,
Galloped to their sure destruction
To be reborn deep below.
Wild creatures, foaming, frenzied,
With tangled manes that flashed
In unwavering fury
Against the red cliffs dashed.

Salt-laden breaths assailed the air,
To mingle with my own,
And overwhelmingly I felt
That I was not alone.
A mighty hand outstretched to stay
Each wave-borne beast that towered,
And all that surging tumult
Into poetry was powered.

The Oaken Gate

The great oak tree had fallen,
Long years had taken toll,
Its branches chopped for firewood
Lay all around its bole.
"There is some useful timber,"
Said the farmer of the land,
"I think I'll use some for a gate,
I'll saw it up by hand."

A strong and heavy wooden gate
Took shape and soon was taken
To the entrance of the field
(To save the farmer's bacon),
Which on four legs and curious
Were often apt to stray
Down the lane beside the hedge
Where fallen apples lay.

Now many were the seasons
The oak tree here had flourished,
And insects in abundance
Acorns and leaves had nourished;
Life saps all were shrivelled
And its trunk now sawed and planed,
And so the field which lent its yield
A new sentinel has gained.

I am a Song

I am a song, I come to you
In blackest night through moods of blue,
Or when dawn lights the eastern sky
Birdsong and breeze will float me nigh.
I am a song, I am temptation
And rouse you from deep contemplation.

I'm in your heart by river's flow
And warm your mind by bonfire's glow.
My highest pitch scales even mountains,
My joyous note tinkles through fountains.
I sing my gentlest through your sadness
And elevate your soul in gladness.
I am a song, I am life's tonic,
I am even supersonic.

Throughout the world I wander far,
Indeed I am its brightest star.
I am the teller of life's story
And catalogue both shame and glory.
I lift your voice to join with me
In celebration of humanity.
My words are heard by every nation,
I am a song – I am creation.

The Lamb

The woodland lane was slushy
As snow and frost lay thawing,
Branches overhead stripped bare
And hungry rooks were cawing;
Ghostly mists hung murkily
And curtained distant scene,
Long past was summer's glory
And springtime's thrusting green.
Dreary, drab and dismal
Described November's day.
What could cheer, this time of year,
Without sun's hopeful ray?
But then beside a gate I paused
To hear a trembling bleat –
A small and snow-white lambkin
Lay close beside my feet.
What change beset the heart and mind
And gave joy resurrection:
God's gift to winter's bleakness,
A newborn lamb's perfection.

Life's Rugged Road

Life's like that,
It picks you up,
Then knocks you flat,
It's a mixture of both joy and woe.
To live full life we undergo
Years of happiness, followed by
Times that make one fret and cry.
Real friends are those, genuine and true
Who in all times are there for you.
If you in turn are staunch and kind
Peace in sadness you will find;
'Though some might snub you – do not heed,
Maybe it's their sad hearts that bleed.
Turn the other cheek and smile,
Forgiveness eases many a mile
Along life's rough and rugged road
And kindness lightens someone's load.
Yes – life's like that!
It picks you up,
Then knocks you flat,
Deal with it as you must;
But try to keep both faith and trust.

Optimism

I leant upon a rustic fence
As light crept from the land,
And in the chilly wind I felt
The touch of winter's hand.
Above, the branches creaked and groaned
As their last leaves were spent,
The prospect held no pleasantness,
Swift homeward I was bent.

But as I hurried down the lane,
A forecast came of spring
As from a barren hazel bush
A robin chanced to sing;
Some optimism in his song
Upon this wintry eve
Made me feel that bird had gained
What man must yet achieve.

Time's Mockery

Never watch that ticking clock,
Its hands seem to move slower.
If you wish to speed it up
Take out the garden mower.
Cut the grass and weed the border,
Put the inside rooms in order;
When next its face you look upon
The awaited lunch hour's come and gone!
Never watch that ticking clock,
It plays tricks with time
Mere man to mock.

The Water Babies

Five water babes one after another
Paddled their way
'Twixt banks of clay,
Close following their father and mother.

These baby ducklings so recently hatched,
Swift learnt to swim,
Saw swallows skim;
But, alas, one a grey heron dispatched.

Of the four ducklings, one then paused to peep
At a green frog,
Squat on a log,
And a great pike pulled him into the deep.

Three fluffy babies were all that were left;
"Keep close my dears,
More danger nears":
As a lean water rat, intent on theft,

Captured another of that little brood;
Now there were two;
But these both grew
To adults – more water babies ensued.

The Garden Guest

My name is Robin, Robin Redbreast;
Because I sport a scarlet vest,
Of which indeed I'm truly proud
(Much smarter than that sparrow crowd!).
I think humans like me the best
As in their garden I am guest
And do not mingle with the rest;
Squabbling starlings, grabbing crows,
I do not associate with those!
The crumbs you scatter out for me
They gobble up so greedily;
So silently among the shrubs,
I search for worms and other grubs,
And as I daily make my quests,
For you reduce those tiresome pests.
You treasure me, this I know
For when wild winter winds do blow,
There is a shelter built for me,
On a shed beneath a tree.
For my services you invest
And in spring there I will nest;
Storms may blow from east or west,
My young shall be your future guests.

The Vital Spark

There's a tiny ray of sunshine
Lying deep within my heart,
And it seldom dims completely,
Though I may feel torn apart
By frustration, grief or worry,
And days seem bleak and dark,
And though that tiny ray may flicker,
Dies not its vital spark.

That tiny ray of sunshine comes
Directly from the Lord;
I feel it and I know it,
Clear as the spoken word,
Sent to me through Nature's voice
And through all creation –
In bird and brook, in flower and tree
Is eternal celebration.

How Good This Earth Could Be

The pen, it has been said,
Is mightier than the sword,
And this we must employ
If peace is to be restored;
Heads of countries shall be swayed
By the petitions of the masses,
Not by sword, by gun or bomb,
The written word surpasses.
No loss of life, no hurt or pain,
No despoiling of surroundings,
No homelessness – no refugees,
No wounded and no foundlings:
Oh that all governments would learn
How good this earth could be
For every living person,
If mankind were truly free
From self-imposed destruction;
Let us write and never cease,
May wisdom ever arbitrate
And wield the key to peace.

The Rock

The rock which lies upon the sand
Was formed by an almighty hand,
The hand that designed each tiny flower
Controls the sea in all its power,
Recycles all the water upon earth,
Gives every living creature birth.
The rock is solid, firm and grounded,
On this should all our ways be founded.
It did not happen just to be –
The rock, or yet the flower or sea,
They were made for this world's glory,
That we may learn the truth – the story
That all creation came to be
From God – a gift for you and me.

The Crow's Lament

Razor-beaked and feather-cloaked,
Upon the fence a gaunt crow croaked;
"I did not ask to be a crow,
For all men hate me, this I know,
Begrudging me their crumbs of bread,
Knowing my nestlings must be fed;
Yet freely strewn are offerings
For many other fluttering wings.

"Blackcap, robin, finch and thrush,
All sing sweetly from the bush;
But that which issues from my throat
I know it is a raucous note.
To scare me, men clap hands or yell,
To be a crow is sometimes hell!
As farmers with loud bangers try
To scare me witless from the sky.

"I did not ask to be a crow,
Why so black? I do not know.
My one good deed – to clear away
Carrion, from the Queen's highway.
Forgive the song I'll not attain,
Forgive my blackened visage plain.
If you will spare some mouldy cheese,
I'll disappear among the trees."

The Dance of Devonshire

I am the dance of Devonshire,
Diverse are my paces,
Slow or fast whatever suits
My mood, my mirth – its places.
I waltz through bluebell woodlands
And the primrosed copse;
Down the hill beside the mill
I move to polka hops.
Then a country dance upon the green,
Beneath the chestnuts spread
Where children oft share merriment
And so the feet are led
To foxtrot, along the riverbank
Until I reach the weir;
My feet join in its rhythm
And engage a faster gear.
Water's splash on rock and stone,
A tap dance brings to mind,
In all of Devon's glorious scene
Fresh dance I always find.
I am the dance of Devonshire,
Be happy! – follow me
Through this inspiring county
Of farmland, moor and sea.

Supreme Plan

Rearrange things though we can,
The earth's not shaped by man.
God's plan is best;
For winging birds a nest,
A sanctuary and rest:
And think – of buttercups in pink,
Or bluebells in bright flame,
It would not be the same:
Gold-studded meadowlands and leas,
Cool copses – bluebell seas
The heart appease.

Rearrange things though we can,
Earth's not ordained by man.
God perfects and patterns all
With a glory to enthral:
Could you – see foliage in blue?
Could any shade surpass
The green of grass?
The verdancy of springtime's surge
Renews an urge – to believe the truth that lives
And daily gives.
And rearrange things all we can,
There is no greater plan.

Time to Wonder

What is this life if full of haste?
No time to spare, no time to waste,
No time to gaze on nature's glory,
No time to linger through life's story,
No time to illustrate its pages
With memories from successive ages.
As this New Year reveals its face
We hope time moves at gentler pace.

That in each day and many an hour
There is space to wonder at a flower,
Time to listen to the trees –
Music conducted by the breeze;
Time to identify by sight
Our feathered friends – their song, their flight,
Time to assimilate the healing
Power, of nature's bounteous dealing.

PlayStations, phones, computer screens,
Have so eclipsed superior scenes,
Which are freely spread worldwide,
Time must be spared to breathe outside,
To enjoy this green and pleasant earth
And learn its gifts of vital worth;
For what is life if full of haste?
'A deal of happiness gone to waste.'

Things That Count

It's the little things in life that count,
Not the greatest bank account,
Not in flashy clothes or style;
But in the unexpected smile
A stranger gives you in the queue,
And knowing someone shares your view.
It's giving time for dearest friends,
For in this way friendship extends.

It's in saying thanks and voicing praise
To those who brighten all our days.
It's listening to a favourite tune
And viewing waves by light of moon.
It's smelling subtle primrose flowers
Or scenting violets after showers.
Yes, it is these little things,
From which true joy and gladness springs.

The Wild Ones

Our garden roses are a joy
And keep us busy in employ;
We spray against black spot and such,
Water and de-head them much,
Cosset them with special food,
Reap our reward when they look good;
But take a stroll in lane or field
And view raw nature's rosy yield:
Dog roses – burnet – scented briar,
The 'wild ones', which all conspire
To ramble through hedge, shrubs and tree,
In a glory of simplicity:
Pink and white, single and sweet,
Unattended yet complete,
Complete in loveliness as great
As those within our garden gate.
June's own gift and every year
For our pleasure they appear.

Devonshire Is Poetry

Devonshire – gentle rolling hills,
Green valleys and heather-covered moorlands,
Shores washed by shimmering, shining sea.
Devon – a glorious celebrated cathedral city
Is yours. Flower-filled hedgerows and fertile land.
Devon, fruitful orchards and colourful gardens,
Coastal rugged rockeries – campions and sea pinks
Overhanging red cliffs. Homely harbours,
Brightly painted boats and wheeling seabirds.
Cornfields of gold and verdant pastures,
Sheep and cattle contentedly grazing.
Village streamlets where children play
And quaint old bridges of rough-hewn stone.
Devonshire is all this and more,
Written indelibly on the hearts who love her
Devon is poetry.

The Watchers

I watched him – watching the sea,
On a sandy shore he stood,
Unconscious he was of me
High above upon the pier,
Watching him – watching the sea;
He seemed to brood, in pensive mood,
As each wave teased his feet
By inches he would retreat;
But continued to stare
With glazed eyes – watching the sea.

Was he an author pondering a plot?
A poet gathering a verse?
An artist imprinting a seascape?
Or a potential suicide at worse?
He stood watching the sea,
Watched closely by me;
But I had to go – so will never know,
Why his close attention, or yet his intention.
I still wonder and in wondering
Am inspired to immortalise this unknown watcher;
Was another watcher watching me,
Watching him – watching the sea?

Far from the Madding Crowd

Far from the madding crowd
And high on a breeze-kissed hill,
Is where I would wish to be
When caught in the overspill
Of people from a crowded bus,
When in the body-crushing mass
Of a jam-packed store,
I would wish to be transported,
To a wild heath-clad moor.
Far from the madding crowd I gain
A respite from the world,
And savour, smell and view
Nature's beauty fresh unfurled;
Within each person lies a need,
For clean earth – blue sky – and space
To be far from the madding crowd awhile,
Rejuvenates and balances all the human race.

Knowing

I taste the incomparable sweetness of springtime,
I breathe the subtle fragrance of wild primroses,
I see the ethereal beauty of cherry blossom,
I hear the tranquil music of the running stream,
I feel the warmth of love all around,
I hold in my hand the spirit of one yet to scale the skies
And gently I revere perfection
– And I am and Heaven is
And every sense is knowing.

I taste a portion of the wisdom of generations,
I breathe my share of the winds of time,
I see the glory in every feature of nature's face,
I hear the harmonious symphony of earth, sea and sky,
I feel the constant pulse of creation,
I hold in my hand a unique fingerprint
And wonder at the amazing complexity of life
– And I am and Heaven is
And every sense is knowing.

Winter's Replenishment

Give a welcome to winter,
Do not dread this time of year;
For this season brings its own beauty,
To replenish the land and to cheer.
Winter waits at the door with a blanket
To spread upon mountain and moor,
Tucking in the folds of the hillside
Restfulness here to restore.

We all love the spring and the summer,
Autumn lends bright shades of its own;
Yet the frosting by streamlet and lake
Is the artwork of winter alone.
Ferns dip whitened fronds to the water,
Frozen dewdrops sparkle the sedge,
Concrete and brick builds are quilted,
There's a softness to every hard edge.

So let us open the door to the winter
And welcome it into our arms,
Although bare-boned the trees,
Their silhouettes please,
Each species holds its own charms.
Sequin-studded are the dry seed heads,
Glittering icicles hang from the roof,
Our Creator has embellished this season,
In sunlight on snow lies the proof.

Blustery Day

Wind is lapping round the lime,
Giving its leaves an anxious time.
It is battering the beech
And pestering both pear and peach.
By the great oak, wind's rage is borne;
And fells too soon a green acorn.

Wind is roaring through wych elm,
Threatening to overwhelm
And the weeping willow sheds
Slender leaves – now torn to shreds.
The dainty trembling aspen tree
Is stirred and shakes constantly.

Silver Birch is wildly spinning,
Its torn foliage swiftly thinning;
Agitated is the ash,
Losing seeds in wind's quick lash.
Bowed hawthorn's fruit is tossed to earth
To feed hungry birds around its girth.

The holly with its prickly touch
Does not mind strong wind so much.
Ripe red berries still are glowing
Even though fierce gales are blowing.
Within the churchyard, the ancient yew
Spreads wide its limbs, so winds pass through.

The Owl's Tale

I am an owl, I flit and fly,
Seeking my prey on earth from sky.
On the evening breeze I glide
On silent wings – for voles might hide –
And future young might hungry be,
As food and home depend on me.
There is seldom time to rest,
As far and wide o'er fields I quest,
To find a suitable cosy place
Wherein to perpetuate my race.
My ancestors long years ago
Never had this problem though.
The ancient barns then to be found,
Sadly these days are not around,
And the places that we sought
Have by builders all been bought
And now are occupied by man
(Barn owls do not like this plan!);
Now scarcely seen on post or gate,
Fewer to meet and choose a mate.
I am an owl – help me, I plea,
Make space among your kind for me,
And please, please, do assist us soon,
That owls might flit neath many a moon.

Lost Meadowlands

I could weep as I see
Our countryside disappearing,
Slowly but insidiously
Concrete replaces clay,
Glass replaces grass,
New towering blocks – vanishing rocks.
Towns nudge downs aside.
Dear countryside which I once roamed,
Where are you going? and how long
Before your sweet meadowlands
Are car parks, multi-stores and roads?
I weep as many others do,
For the wild meadows that I knew.
I remember the flowers, butterflies, ladybirds
And the honeyed sweetness of it all.
Cranesbill, clover, coltsfoot, campions
And the overhanging hedges, thick with verdancy.
Briar rose, bryony, honeysuckle and hops,
A haven for our precious birds and wildlife.
I weep for this irreplaceable treasure.

Birds in a Storm
(a pantoum)

A wee wren and a rook
Crash-landed down together
And sat close in a crook
In an ash tree in wild weather.

Crash-landed down together
As the storm winds blew them there
In an ash tree in wild weather
Ill-matched were the pair.

As the storm winds blew them there
Both be-ruffled and so cold,
Ill-matched were the pair –
The small and sweet, the big and bold.

Both be-ruffled and so cold,
To the blown bough holding fast,
The small and sweet, the big and bold
At the mercy of the blast.

To the blown bough holding fast
And sat close in a crook
At the mercy of the blast,
A wee wren and a rook.

Untrodden Snow

Whiter than the whisper of wind among the poplars,
Planting its kisses on newly felted leaves,
Whiter than ox-eye daisies carpeting the wayside,
Or dancing in profusion
On the upland leas;
Whiter – so much whiter is the snow than these.

Whiter than the petals, flung from the blossomed cherry
Or the wild anemones beneath the woodland trees;
Whiter than the pale moonlight, on barley harvest ripe,
Whiter than a wavelet's foam
Surfing the shimmering seas;
Whiter – much, much whiter is the snow than these.

Whiter than the swans along the waterways,
Whiter than the may hung on springtime thorn;
Whiter than a surpliced choir,
Or doves that haunt the topmost spire,
Whiter than a lamb newborn,
Whiter – whiter still, untrodden snow at morn.

Master of the Plot

I am a weed and I will grow
Up through the plants you cherish so.
I do not say, "Oh, beg your pardon,
May I seed into your garden?"
I sow my offspring on the breeze
And root them down just where I please,
And I find the choicest spot,
Where you wish a weed was not.
I deprive phlox, lily and aster
Of food and space, for I am master;
If you try to kill my root,
You also destroy their living shoot.
My name is Dandelion – and so
I proliferate when winds do blow.
I am a weed, I have succeeded,
Right in the plot which you've just weeded.

Seagulls at Shaldon

Callers of the raucous cry,
Eyeing humans from on high,
Stealers of the luncheon snacks,
Perched upon the chimney stacks.
Holidaymakers on the beach
Closely watched are all and each;
Robbers of their fish and chips,
Scavengers of the rubbish tips,
Oft regarded as real pests
When they claim our roof for nests;
Delighting us when soaring high,
Purest white 'gainst azure sky.
'Angelic loveliness on wing' –
Then we forgive you anything,
For seaside holidays would seem dull
Without sight and sound of the seagull.

A Country Dog Show

A Poodle in a knitted skin,
A Dachshund like a rolling pin,
A Whippet thinnest of the thin,
Which will the judge proclaim to win?
A King Charles rather overfed,
A Boxer with an outsized head,
A Hound refusing to be led,
The judge begins to scratch his head!
Red Setters by the dozen there,
A tall Afghan with 'blow-dry' hair,
An odd-shaped dog which must be rare,
The judge has risen from his chair.

<u>Class One</u> – The most appealing eyes:
The plump King Charles takes the prize,
Around his neck his mistress ties
A blue rosette, and a treat supplies.

<u>Class Two</u> – The waggiest tail in sight:
Owners persuade with all their might
To wag to left and wag to right,
And so all the dogs excite!
The winner of this class for sure
Was a big black Labrador.

<u>Class Three</u> – The dog resembling most
His owner: this a few could boast.
A boy and Dachshund brown as toast
Were certain winners at this post.

<u>Class Four</u> – The dog the judge thought best:
A Collie in a white-front vest,
Alert and healthy passed the test,
Though every dog outshone the rest
In their owner's doting eyes,
Each special pet deserved a prize.
Amazing how quickly time goes by
And how many laughs dog shows supply.

While I – Even I

Niagara's waters foam and tumble,
While I with tangled shoelace fumble.
A gigantic iceberg's being carved
While I see a fruit pie fairly halved.
Saharan sands whip to a storm
While I put signature to form.
Himalayan peaks don misty shrouds,
While I am lost midst shopping crowds.
The mighty Amazon outpours
While I restock my chosen stores.
Pacific currents heave and surge
While I my cake ingredients merge.
The wondrous Barrier Reef expands
While I cook lunch – spaghetti strands.
This global sphere spins at a rate
While I repaint the garden gate.
Over all this I've no control;
Yet surely I must have a soul
From which appreciation flows
And births poetry and prose,
That with vast wonders – even I,
Through such small acts may signify.

Flower-Arranging Classes in November

She taught us all to look and see
The beauty in each shrub and tree,
To use our eyes and so perceive
The different texture of each leave;
She trained our senses to observe
The possibility in a curve
Of many a dead and fallen branch,
And to spare more than a glance
At a common garden weed,
To which before we gave no heed.
She taught us this and also made
Us conscious of both light and shade,
Of hues which complement and blend,
Of contour, contrast, line and bend.
She showed us how to grace a room
With subtle touch of bud and bloom,
She lent our hands a certain skill,
To create beauty and fulfil
Within ourselves an inner need;
For with such skills we're blessed indeed.
Cold, bleak weeks in dull November
Have given much happiness to remember.
Thank you, teacher, very much
For passing on your magic touch.

The Lonesome Pine

I stand alone within a field,
Amidst the grass and sedges.
My kin and other leafy trees
Far-flung beyond the hedges.
So when the breeze comes whispering,
I have no friends to share
Its delightful secrets, gathered
From land and air;
I stand alone for I began
When a bird dropped seed,
And it became my lot to be
A lonesome pine indeed.

I stand alone when north winds blow
And earth grows cold and bare,
My relatives crowd side by side,
Each other's shelter share;
But when the springtime comes around
And my boughs are sun-caressed,
Many songsters seek a home
So my lonesome life is blessed.
I know my offspring will be birthed
In future germinations,
When nestlings fledge, take of my seed
To disperse in new locations.

A Pig's Reprieve at Pennymoor

I am a pig, I squeal and grunt
To get at food, for I'm the runt;
Last of the litter to get out,
So do not know what life's about.
My brothers and my sisters too,
Have discovered where the milk comes through.
It seems they all have found their place,
But for me there is no space.
The farmer comes and shakes his head,
Says, "This one must be bottle-fed."

He picks me up, I squeal with fright,
But soon I'm fed and feel all right.
I'm lucky to be at Pennymoor
(Quite near Tiverton for sure).
Now though I started out all wrong,
In weeks to come I grow more strong.
Back to my siblings I am taken,
The farmer says, "Unfit for bacon."
He smooths my head – I give a grunt,
I think I'm glad to be a runt.

Happy Wanderers

Root by root and stem by stalk
The ox-eye daisies took a walk –
Along the motorway's vast verge
They progressed forward in a surge;
Dressed in virgin bridal white,
To human eyes a wondrous sight.
Into the wayside fields they wandered,
Freely there much seed they squandered,
Where scarlet poppies joined their dance,
The English summer to enhance;
From Devonshire's hills to Dorset's dales
Their simple loveliness regales.

Gone with the Wind

Gone with the wind are the autumn leaves,
As are the swallows from under the eaves.
Gone is the sunlight as winter hovers,
And fields are visited by plovers;
The redwings and the fieldfares swarm
In the orchard near the farm,
To feast upon the fallen fruit.
Cock pheasants call and sportsmen shoot.
Gone with the wind are summer's dreams,
As winter with its icy schemes
Chases lingering warmth away;
But 'Tomorrow is another day.'

Springtime Blesses All

Awakening woods cast off grey hoods
As early sun lends its smile,
And dons green bonnets, inspiring sonnets
Our spirits to beguile.

Beneath the trees, lately at ease,
The hedgehog uncurls again,
And stirring life is roused and rife
In every woodland lane.

Bluebells thrust through, soon to paint blue
Each glade and forest floor,
Like inland seas – alluring bees;
Gorse-braided is Exmoor.

Primroses peep – maternal sheep
Their wandering lambkins call;
Birds sing with zest and weave their nests
As springtime blesses all.

Christmas Eve
(a pantoum)

The moon shone clear and bright,
The owls were on call,
Carols echoed through the night,
Berried holly decked the hall.

The owls were on call,
Young lambs flocked together,
Berried holly decked the hall,
Ferns mimicked snow-white feathers.

Young lambs flocked together
As the Christmas star smiled down,
Ferns mimicked snow-white feathers,
White was the fir tree's gown.

As the Christmas star smiled down
People's prayers ascended,
White was the fir tree's gown;
Peace on earth descended.

People's prayers ascended,
Carols echoed through the night,
Peace on earth descended,
The moon shone clear and bright.

The Stricken Ash at Bickleigh

I am a tree – my name is Ash,
Among my twigs I feel a splash
Of rain; but sadly now
It will not replenish leaves on bough,
Which all have fallen far too soon
(I cannot blame the harvest moon).
There is a sickness in our trees,
Perhaps carried on the breeze,
Maybe insects are to blame?
Within my bark I feel aflame.
My withering keys so sere and dark
Are strewn around my homeland park.
Unfit to germinate and raise
Young trees to grace earth's future days.
I feel so ill, I feel despair,
With my species dying everywhere.
Will scientific minds conspire
To save each ash from axe and fire?
I am an ash, a graceful tree.
Will I become a memory?

The Last Rosebud

Imprisoned in an icy cagé,
Galmpton's last rosebud of the year
Will never bow on flora's stage,
Or scent surrounding sphere.
Blue tits search among its briars
For insects, all in vain,
Entombed alike are aphids
In glassy frozen rain.

Why did this rosebud linger long
Until frost-bound December?
Could it not have joined the throng
That brightened warm September?
Now those folded petals
Will never blush to red
As winter spreads its blanket round
And sends all blooms to bed.

Granny's Old Black Crock

Granny's old crock was iron black
And hung on a crook in the chimney stack,
Beneath it blazed a fire of logs,
Within it simmered beef or hog's
Knuckles – tripe or mutton stew,
With onions, carrots, turnips too.
The pied cat slept in sweet repose
Close by the fire, but twitched his nose
As savoury smells imbued the air,
The source of which he hoped to share.

Beside the crock there hung a kettle,
In the same black heavy metal,
Each essentials, large and weighty
For Gran to lift, when nearing eighty.
Such hard work those old folk suffered,
By no mod cons were their tasks buffered:
Every pudding, pie or cake
Was mixed by hand to steam or bake.
Each day the grate was cleaned and fired
(No help of any kind was hired).

Fetching logs and chopping sticks,
Hard times indeed! – yet eighty-six
Was the age dear Granny made
Ere to Witheridge farewell she bade.
I often think of my loving Gran
On viewing a lightweight pot or pan,
Shining bright in stainless steel,
And visualise her chop and peel
Vegetables to make a stock
For cooking in her old black crock.

Enchantment

Abracadabra
Brings magic to the mind,
Colours of the rainbow,
Dancers and design.
Enchantment in midsummer,
Fairies by the lake,
Goblins sat at toadstools eating
Honeysuckle cake,
Ice cream sweet as may bloom,
Jelly rosy reds,
Kingcupped in the goblets of
Lovely flower heads.
Magic days of sunshine,
Nights deep velvet blue,
Owls flit by moonlight with
Pixie passengers too.
Queen Mab gives a banquet of
Refreshments quite divine,
Strawberries crushed for sorbet
Thyme blossom distilled wine:
Under feathery fern fronds,
Verdant grass soft to the feet,
Wind amid the woodbine sings;
Xylophones – the woodpeckers beat;
Yarrow scents pillows for small fays,
Zephyrs fan dreams of spellbound days.

The Message of the Rose

A pink and perfect rose I eyed,
As it waved in perfumed pride;
It made me think that such design
Could not be wrought by me or mine.
Maybe I could achieve its shape,
Or a shading of its colour ape;
But not in paint or porcelain
Could I its beauty full attain.
Not in silver, gold or glass
Could I its glossy leaves surpass.
To think, this from a cutting grew,
A living treasure for to view,
And in the viewing of, inspire
A spark of our Creator's fire.
So the message of the rose
Is carried on the wind that blows,
And echoed from the tallest tree,
God created this for you and me.

The Days of Steam
(Exe Valley Line)

Seven country girls rode daily,
Upon the branch line into town,
To earn their bread and butter
And per week save half a crown:
The steam train that conveyed them
Huffed, puffed and whistled on the way,
Beside the Exe along the meadows,
Shadowing all with breath of grey.

Seven country girls were knitting
As they travelled to and fro,
Plain and purl, Fair Isle patterns
Into scarves and mitts to grow.
Pullovers, cosy sweaters,
Twinsets, cardigans and gloves;
Christmas presents for their families,
Birthday offerings for young loves.

Seven country girls ne'er wasted time
Upon the old steam train,
Read the classics while they knitted,
Exercising hands and brain;
Firemen, guards and engine drivers
Soon knew every girl by name,
Now and then a mild flirtation,
Now and then a waiting game.

One country girl mapped out her future,
Travelling on the old steam train.
She 'engaged' an engine driver,
Her daily journey not in vain.
Marriage was proposed – accepted,
On the platform in the snow.
Gone now tracks and railway stations,
Where steam trains puffed, wild bluebells blow.

One country girl with her offspring
Still walks the track where once she rode,
Counting memories like treasures,
Appraising each as they unfold,
Thinking of the steam and stitches
And garments fashioned long since worn,
Immortalising time and travel
In 'The days of steam' reborn.

The Village Churchyard

Over lost loved ones spring has spread
A quilt of gold upon earth's bed,
As myriad celandines unfold
Petals bright, brilliant, bold,
Reflecting early sunshine's rays –
A sight to lighten lonesome days.
They sleep with beauty all around,
In our churchyard's hallowed ground;
A mistle thrush has made a nest
And robins sing above their rest.
Primroses and lady's smocks
Mingle with plantains and docks,
Providing food for butterflies –
These lend some solace to our sighs.
Herein they lie at peace and free
From all which troubles you and me.

Bleak House

Its only shelter where it stood
Was a stunted pine,
It felt the spirit of every wind,
Its whirl, its wail, its whine;
The west wind lashed into its face;
The east wind tore its back,
The fierce onslaught from the north
Sought every open crack
Around the windows and the door;
The old house surely knew,
From prolonged exposure,
Which way the four winds blew.
Its only occupant, one old man
Who had lost both child and spouse;
Bleak was his outlook and his home,
So aptly named 'BLEAK HOUSE'.

Gather Such Treasure

I love to roam a Devon shore,
Its dunes and hollows to explore,
To hold its treasures in my hand,
As sugar-fine – some golden sand,
Or glimpse a pebble black as jet
Shining in the wavelets wet;
From north to south along our coast
There's diversity of which to boast.

I love to stand on Devon's shores,
Where taste and feel of spray restores
And animates the jaded mind;
Some hidden jewel I'm sure to find.
A shell as delicate and pale
Pink, as a newborn baby's nail,
Or purest white of such perfection
They move the mind to deep reflection.

Tributaries from the moors
Deposit colours to our shores,
Influenced by plants and weather,
Pebbles hold the tints of heather,
Lichens and leaves from upland trees
Lend pigments to our estuaries,
While over this delightful scene
Heaven's watch has ever been.

Come stroll these lovely shores with me
And feel the pull of poetry,
In cry of gull, in sound of surf,
The seaweed's tang, its beaded girth
Laid like a necklace from the deep,
Mementoes in our hearts to keep
When age and infirmities hold sway;
Gather such treasure while you may.

A Village Owl and Pussycat Tale

A local owl and pussycat
Met one day by chance.
Owl was perched in a hornbeam,
When puss climbed to the same branch;
They took a fancy to each other,
Owl thought the cat's fur divine,
Pussy stroked owl's soft feathers
And purred, "On what do you dine?"
"Worms and small frogs found beneath logs,"
Replied owl in a trice,
"Young birds and shrews; but if I could choose,
My favourite food is just mice."

Pussy pondered awhile,
Then, with a broad smile, said,
"Mice are my favourite too,
Shall we go hunting together?"
Owl agreed with a loud "Twit-a-whoo."
They searched far and wide,
But not one mouse was espied,
What were hungry lovers to do?
So, to save further fuss, they boarded a bus,
To collect some mice from the zoo.

How astonished the pair on arriving there,
To see so many mice in a row,
Mice of all ages at home in their cages,
Brown, grey, and white as the snow,
Long-tailed, short-tailed, thin mice and fat;
But all locked in securely, which they couldn't get at.
To avoid any pillage, they returned to their village
On the X46 from the zoo.
Again hunting they went; but their supper's content
Was one scrawny frog and a shrew.
If somewhere out there, you chance on the pair
And notice they both have grown thinner,
Sympathise with their plight of less prey every night,
And invite them to share Christmas dinner.

On the Line

Swifter than swallows, swifter than hares,
Pass sleepy herds who seem unawares:
Along by the meadows, where woolly sheep graze
On a diet of grass – in early morn's haze.
The sun is a-peeping just over the hill
Where folk in a cottage are breakfasting still.
Here is a river in meandering flow
And there is a small copse with autumnal glow.
Close by a brook a heron is keeping
Watch for a fish, while a sly fox is creeping
Low by a hedgerow, in daily habit
Hoping to snatch a pheasant or rabbit.
Tickety-tick and clackety-clack,
Now there's a bank close by the track
Be-strung with clematis wild and free,
Seed silvered with dewdrops and climbing a tree;
Next a patchwork of fields, stitched together by hedges,
Large grassy spaces and wetlands with sedges.
There is a churchyard right by the line
And a small village church with a spire quite fine.
Trees varied and lovely populate every glade
In russet and red and of rich golden shade.
There is so much to give pleasure on hillside and down;
But the journey's now ending as we approach town.
Tickety-tick and clackety-clack,
We've yet to enjoy the ride going back.
The train is now braking; but again we'll be taking
Future trips when it's fine
On this great Tarka Line.

The Lights of Life

I wander distant as a star
In my own space – companions far
And though I sometimes faintly shine,
Little of this light is mine;
But reflected from on high,
Along with many a tear and sigh,
And it is my lot to share
With miller, maid, or millionaire,
Some of this light, to reconcile
All, in poetry, in song and smile,
That other wandering mortals may
Feel less lonesome on life's way.

I wander distant as a star,
Mourning the loss both near and far
Of friends and loved ones that I've known,
Who now upon a higher throne
No longer need reflected light,
The light is theirs and theirs the might,
All earthly talents magnified;
Their hands from mundane tasks untied.
Why should I mourn? for they are free
In their own space eternally;
Their lights of life shine clear and bright,
Consolation is a starry night.

Celebrations

There are special celebrations,
We can name them one by one,
Weddings, anniversaries
And new lives just begun;
Yet we can find a reason
To celebrate each day,
From the breaking of dawn's first light,
To sunset's vibrant ray.
We can celebrate all nature,
Its complex changing scene,
The revelation of the springtime,
With its fresh translucent green,
The shafts of first pale sunlight
Among the tender leaves
And joy of reborn birdsong,
From woodland, hedge and eaves.

We can celebrate our gardens
Within those sun-blessed hours,
When colours have erupted
In a multi-blaze of flowers,
As every bloom gives forth
Its many glorious gifts
Of perfect form and sweet perfume
(How one's spirit lifts).

We can celebrate our coastline
And the changing mood of seas,
The winding silver rivers
Enriching vales and leas.

We can celebrate our moorlands,
The spacious wild outdoors,
Their panoramic beauty
And rugged granite tors;
When purpled with bell heather
And braided gold with gorse,
How can we fail to celebrate
Vitality's resource?
We can celebrate our friendships
With those we love and trust,
Life is a celebration –
So celebrate we must!

Heart's Truth

When spirit seeks spirit and wisdom ignites
A spark in the writer, it exhorts and excites,
And some work of beauty is bound to be born,
A glimpse given wonder of earth's primal dawn.

When one has been sought and word has been given
The mind is eclipsed, propelled, guided, driven,
Naturally rhymed, excelled and surpassed;
Although dissected and judged it is seldom outclassed.

When spirit finds wisdom, graduation will be
Though the poet might hold no academic degree;
For in real poetry the ultimate goal
Is the heart's truth and freedom of soul.

The freedom that fears not trouble or sorrow,
A freedom that voices the hope for tomorrow,
Freedom that vanquishes evil and wrong –
Such freedom births culture through poem and song.

A Wartime Memory
(Happy Pigs)

My parents kept pigs throughout the war years
Which kept us laughing – then brought us to tears;
They recycled our food waste, with barley meal mixed
And when their lives ended our menus were fixed.
With bacon for breakfast, and roast pork for dinner,
Crisp chitterlings for supper (each meal a winner!).
Our pigs knew no cruelty, their ending was swift,
The butcher employed, did it all in a jiff.

Their lives had been happy, in a clean strawy sty,
In a grassy green mead, with a stream running by;
When summers were hot, pigs wallowed in this,
With contented grunts expressing their bliss.
Some may recoil at the truth in this verse,
But remember, some canines are today treated worse.

Village Barber/Bell-Ringer

My Uncle Frank, cut hair he did,
But only at weekends,
When village lads from Witheridge
Came up the road – his friends.
They would sit in Granny's old back house
And patiently wait their turn,
While I sat quiet as a mouse
(A great deal for to learn!).

Now Uncle Frank was never trained
As a barber – this is true;
Yet somehow he had a knack
To cut a shipshape crew.
Some came with blonde and curled locks,
Or hair straight, thick and black.
However shabbily they had arrived,
They were smarter going back.

There was a deal of laughter
Among the customers and him.
(He only charged a bob a job
So his profit was quite slim.)
Sometimes he would receive a tip,
(Sixpence, he gave to me,
With which I'd buy some pear drops,
Or a doughnut for my tea).

Uncle Frank was a lovely man,
He was everybody's friend.
At forty-nine it was too soon
For his kindly life to end.
He lies at peace in Thelbridge now,
Beneath St David's tower,
And the bells that he once rang
Still peal for service hour.

Grandmother's Bed

My grandmother's bed was too large for herself,
So she took her a husband to share,
There, as a bride, she slept by his side
Every night, on climbing the stair;
Through rain, wind and rime
Sixty years was the time
The old couple more closely grew.
They raised seven sons – not the only ones,
For they also had daughters – two!

But one night changed it all,
For an angel did call
To take dear old grandad away;
The family grieved, but truly believed
They would all meet again some day.
Now my grandmother's bed was too large for herself,
So she invited her grandchild to stay
For holiday times – when old songs and rhymes
Were shared during night-time and day.

Now that child is full-grown, with young of her own,
Those memories live in her heart.
Although Gran is long dead, she remembers the bed,
Snow-white sheets and warm blankets a part.
My grandmother's bed, its springs and its head,
Have all been recycled somewhere;
Yet such precious thought, now has been caught
In a poem the writer must share.

A Most Precious Partridge

She was plump, yet small and pretty,
With hair ripe chestnut brown,
And eyes as bright as midnight stars,
Her forehead wore no frown;
She always kept so active,
Raising ducklings and young chicks,
Never went on holiday, to the seaside or the flicks;
Spent many hours picking peas
And shelling them to freeze.
Her husband was a farmer, so they knew no life of ease.

Now this was our Aunt Edith,
Though we scarcely used this name,
For to all of us who loved her
'Auntie Partridge' she became.
No other name could suit her more
(Partridges these days are few!),
Such sweet delightful country birds,
Just like the aunt we knew;
Gentle and unselfish throughout her busy life,
Her deserved rest – now Heaven sent
For this mother, sister, wife.

Back to Basics

My mother had a wooden spoon,
Which had battered much and beaten
The ingredients from the larder,
To produce all that was eaten.
Christmas puddings, rich with fruit,
Sage stuffing for the goose,
Yorkshire puds. On Sundays
Custard and chocolate mousse.
It stirred the mince for cottage pie,
The gravy for lamb stew,
It stayed strong for years and years
Until her lifetime flew.

Now I keep that wooden spoon
In my cupboard drawer;
And it is seldom used today
For I use a whisk much more,
A blender for the vegetables,
To make good soup real quick
And for a rich and spicy cake
The food mixer does the trick;
But if one day, with cooking planned,
The electricity goes wrong,
Out must come Mum's wooden spoon
And I revive her stirring song.

Back to basics in an age
When gadgets are the thing,
Essential fundamentals –
Our hands plus wood and string.

Like an Ember

How can one not be inspired
To be by poetry lit and fired?
With such beauty all around,
From river, sea – from sight and sound.
The mind an inner camera takes
Snaps of landscapes, mountains, lakes
To be developed sometime, when
Pictures come in words from pen.

This is how true poetry
Comes to you, from such as me,
Nothing clever – nothing planned;
But like an ember, gently fanned,
Slowly becomes a warming fire,
Earth's natural glory will inspire
And I thank powers that be which give
Embryonic thoughts, so words might live.

The Spirit of the River

There is never an end to a river,
Even when it reaches the sea,
For the eddies and swirls of its waters
Retain immortal land memories;
There's the green of the trees in its flowing,
And the sweet wholesome breath of the wheat,
The fragrance of meadowland flowers
And a dark undercurrent of peat;
It carried the glitter of sunlight,
The reflection of summer blue sky,
Murmuring voices of countryside
Are gathered from far off or nigh.
Colour and perfume, movement and sound
Are absorbed in slow or swift motion:
There is never an end to a river
For its spirit lives on in the ocean.

Bird Talk

I am a tiny feathered bird,
Perched high upon a bough,
Below me black and horned there stands
A creature known as cow;
It chews and chews at grass all day,
It is awkward, loud and big,
I'm glad I am a little bird,
To fly from twig to twig.

I am a bird, I am building
My nest, my young to sleep;
Beneath my home there grazes
A creature known as sheep;
It's fat and rather stupid
(For young it makes no nest);
With joy I sing, for this is spring,
To be a bird is best.

I am a bird, I am bathing
My plumage in a stream,
Within the water clear there darts
A trout, a perch, a bream,
Creatures of the water world,
Commonly known as fish;
To change with them my airy life
Would never be my wish.

I am a bird, I am searching
For insects on the gorse;
Near me, flicking flies away,
Is a creature known as horse,
Who is used to transport humans
(Which I think is quite absurd);
I'm glad I'm me, I'm glad I'm free,
I'm glad I am a bird.

So Great a Heritage

Our churches are beautiful,
Great monuments to bygone praise,
And towers of strength in present days,
Sure hope for all our future ways –
So great a heritage.

By craftsmen skilled their beauty wrought,
Where teachers of God's word have taught,
And many to repentance brought –
The churches of old England.

Here folk have worked, sung hymns and prayed,
Tapestries wove and flowers arrayed,
Wept, laughed and steadfast faith displayed
Within these hallowed walls.

Our churches are beautiful
May we this generation keep
Them so – as those, who round them sleep,
Did likewise toil, that we might reap
So great a heritage.

Remembering Diana

She will not be forgotten,
For she shed a ray of gold
Upon the destitute and homeless,
The disabled, sick and old;
She also loved all children,
Regardless of their skin,
And hugged, kissed and caressed them
As though they were her kin:
Now the love she freely shared
With all peoples of mankind
Is being returned a thousandfold
To her dear sons left behind;
And with our love and comfort
We pray God they will find
Together with her memory –
Inspiration – peace of mind.
May God grant our dear princess
A sleep of blessed repose,
For she was the true epitome
Of a lovely English rose.

When Wild Cherries Blossom

Oh to be in Devon
As April comes along;
Whoever walks in Devon
Will sing a heartfelt song,
For the beauty of the springtime
Across the greening land,
And a stardust of small daisies
Strewn by April's hand.

Oh to be in Devon
When April here arrives;
Whoever dwells in Devon
Adds a richness to their lives;
When the wild cherries blossom
And pollened alders swing,
A stroll beside the River Exe
Will inspiration bring.

Oh to be in Devon
When April wields her brush
And paints anew the patterns
On chaffinch, lark and thrush;
And raises high her baton
To conduct their sweet spring song,
To be at home in Devon –
Then, all wanderers must long.

Heart of a Rose

White ones bring visions of my wedding bouquet
And the church decorated for our special day;
Golden ones hold happy memories too,
Remember we planted some, just me and you?
While pink ones, tight-budded into a curl
Remind me of the hands of our first baby girl.
Red ones say I love you, in so many ways,
Velvet and fragrant in gardens ablaze,
There are more memories than one may suppose
Hidden within the heart of a rose.

The Wind in the Willows

The wind sang in the willows
And the sun smiled on the pond:
In white muslin billows,
Freshly washed and donned,
The clouds danced minuets above
The pleasant springtime scene,
While the wind sang in the willows
Wherein the buntings preened.
A frog croaked neath the reed mace,
Gold kingcups blazed in glory;
And a writer by the pond
Began a children's story:
He wrote of wild creatures
In leafy beds with mossy pillows,
And his characters awoke to life
As the wind sang in the willows.

West Country Moorlands

Wild as the creatures
Which over them run;
Mellowed by blessings
Of sudden bright sun,
Craggy rocks – wide mossy stretches,
Whortleberry, gorse,
Entangled with vetches;
Wind inhales the perfume of heather,
Which both ling and bell
Exhale together,
Sweetening the air all around;
And purple painting
The wide moorland ground.
How lucky the rambler
In this part of the world
To stand on these heights
And behold such glory unfurled.

Ticket to Ride

I've got a ticket to ride!
For a senior some compensation,
Free journeys, yards from my door,
To bus depot, or to train station,
And each ride is a pleasurable thing,
Especially when year's at the spring.
No need to focus on highways,
Eyes may wander the byways,
And reap in their gold,
As oilseed crops unfold;
While trees overspill
Fresh blooms on the hill.
Yes! I've got a ticket to ride,
And who will sit down by my side?
A stranger unknown
To a new friend oft grown,
Exchanging one's views,
Or the latest big news;
New outlooks to learn,
At each twist and turn,
Sharing one's load
As we traverse the road;
Yes! I've got a ticket to ride
Through idyllic countryside.

Did They Know?

The moon's clear face was bright to view,
In the cold and sparkling air,
Hard-iced were ploughed furrows
As the fox crept to her lair,
Wherein the family waited
For her warmth's return;
Nestled neath the ivy leaves
(Human eyes could not discern),
A lone red-breasted robin,
Beneath the cowshed eaves.

Near the top of a great pine tree
A squirrel tucked away,
Wrapping his tail around his head,
Real cosy in his drey.
Rabbits in warrens safe and snug,
The dormouse in her nest;
Moonlight shone above,
Christmas Eve was at its best.

Fir trees were frost-encrusted,
Bells pealed to greet the dawn;
Did all these wild creatures sense
That their Maker blessed this morn?

New Year

New as a babe's first breath
Upon the air,
New as untrodden snow,
New thought – new care.

New as dawn's waking light,
As day unknown,
New as a fledgling's flight,
New seed – new sown.

New as a page unmarked
By careless hands,
New as a friendship born,
New hopes – new plans.

New as love's stirring flame,
Untarnished bright,
New Year came in
And set the world aright.